H
Secure Woman

40-day devotional

Catherine Butcher

Foreword by Jeannette Barwick

Published 2006 by CWR, Waverley Abbey House, Waverley Lane,
Farnham, Surrey GU9 8EP, England.

See back of book for list of National Distributors.

Concept development, editing, design and production by CWR

Cover image: Getty/Stone+

Printed in Finland by WS Bookwell

ISBN-13: 978-1-85345-391-5
ISBN-10: 1-85345-391-9

Contents

Introduction

Week 1
Know your own heart

Week 2
Where does your security lie?

Week 3
Knowing God's heart

Week 4
Facing hard facts

Week 5
Removing the roadblocks

Week 6
Moving forward

Week 7
Believing, becoming and being secure

Week 8
Developing good relationships

Introduction

One of the joys of my Christian life has been to meet and work with women in many and varied settings and, with the help of the Holy Spirit, to gain a special understanding of how women tick – myself included! Over thirty years, the ministry into which God gradually led me has taken me to four continents and provided a wealth of experience. Through it I have come to realise that the issue of insecurity, though not of course unique to women, is certainly problematic for us, not least in the spiritual dimension of our lives.

The teaching at the heart of How to be a Secure Woman is fundamental to the full range of CWR's teaching and ministry, which you may already have encountered. It is the subject of the women's seminar we present extensively, both in the UK and in a number of other countries, and also its companion eight-session workbook, which is particularly, though not exclusively, suited to group use. Study groups using the material have been set up in many churches while others have hosted the seminar. I was recently encouraged to be told that a women's conference in Frankfurt on this theme was 'one of the highlights of our church's year and made a lasting impact advancing Christ's kingdom'. At the end of this devotional are some more testimonies from women whose lives have been transformed by this teaching.

The issues tackled in How to be a Secure Woman are real, rooted in the everyday experience of women in all their diversity everywhere, and require a practical response. The devotional to which I am now introducing you stands apart from the other resources as more personal, being designed to encourage individual exploration and sustained reflection in pursuit of the common goal: a richer and deeper relationship with God.

I pray that this booklet will prove a valuable resource in helping you to find security as a woman in the only place that it can truly be found – Jesus Christ.

For I am convinced that neither death nor life … nor anything else in all creation, will be able to separate us from the love of God that is in Christ Jesus our Lord.

(Rom. 8:38–39)

Jeannette Barwick
Head of Women's Ministries

God knows
my heart

Jeremiah 17:7–10

'He will be like a tree planted by the water … It has no worries in a year of drought and never fails to bear fruit.' (v.8)

How can I be a secure woman? If only I could flick a switch to know instant, unshakeable security. But life and faith are not like that. Even the most outwardly secure woman is a work in progress. We discover the extent of our security through the challenges of change and difficulty.

When I first met Jennifer Rees Larcombe she was confined to a wheelchair. A mother of six, she'd been struck down by serious illness. 'I felt as if our happiness had been smashed forever,' she said. Years later we met again – she'd been miraculously healed and was leading a conference with her husband. Then her marriage broke down. Again, she had to put the pieces of her broken life into God's hands: 'When we are willing to hand Him all those broken pieces, He can begin to rebuild us,' she says, and with hindsight she adds, 'The marriage break-up was one of the most helpful things God could have allowed.'

Jen has had to learn through pain and hardship that security doesn't lie in being healthy or married. Lasting security comes when we trust God. Then, like the man Jeremiah describes, we can live fruitful lives whatever our circumstances.

We might think we are secure, but we are easily deceived by our own fickle hearts. Difficulties show our weaknesses and challenge us to change as we learn to trust God. There are no short cuts, but God will not test you beyond your endurance (1 Cor. 10: 13).

Even though she was imprisoned in the Nazi concentration camp where she later died, Betsy ten Boom asserted: 'There is no pit so deep that God's love is not deeper still.'

 Switch your focus to God: His character, His purpose for your life, His promises. Praise Him for His strength, His reliability, His love. Ask for His help to see your life as He sees it: a work in progress. Look to Him for your security.

Who is the greatest?

Matthew 18:1–5

'… unless you change and become like little children, you will never enter the kingdom …' (v.3)

Having a career was the sixties' answer to women's demands for equality. Forty years on, and many have-it-all career women acknowledge that the stress of juggling family and full-time work is too much. But high-flying careers and other achievements – even gourmet-success in the kitchen – give many women the status and security they crave.

Jesus' disciples were status-seekers too. When asked 'Who is the greatest?' Jesus showed them that they needed to have a completely different way of thinking. He pointed to a child.

Children can be even more competitive than adults, so what point was Jesus making? Compared with adults, children are happy to be dependent, but they need more than a homework-helper, personal shopper or chauffeur. Children are most secure when they are loved, affirmed, encouraged ... and cuddled. Children can live with a minimum of most things, but psychologists recognise that they need love.

Perhaps it is this basic requirement that Jesus was homing in on: children want to be loved. Good loving imposes boundaries to keep them safe; good loving is tough enough to include discipline; it is also 'patient' and 'kind'. 'It always protects, always trusts, always hopes, always perseveres' and 'never fails' (1 Cor. 13:4,7–8).

That's the security God offers us if we become like little children. It is not like the security offered by careers and achievements. It lasts when the arrival of a baby means a job becomes impossible. Or if health gives way and we have to give up work. Or if divorce, redundancy or retirement means we have to move or go without. Or if an elderly parent needs full-time care and our dreams are set aside.

God gives us women a job description: to give Him glory. Married or single, with or without children, it's a challenge which suits all circumstances and offers eternal job security.

 Thank You Father for loving me, protecting me, persevering with me. Your patience and kindness amaze me.

New order

John 2:1–11

'Do whatever he tells you.' (v.5)

How do you introduce yourself – with your job description, as your parents' daughter, your husband's wife, your children's mother? Do you draw your identity from your role in life, or is your identity securely rooted in your relationship with God?

At the wedding in Cana, Jesus might have been introduced as 'Mary's son' or 'the carpenter's son'. But the occasion marked a turning point in Jesus' life and revealed the source of His identity as well as His glory.

Jewish mothers are often mocked for being manipulative and domineering, though they are also respected for their central, life-giving role in Jewish families. We know that Jesus was obedient to His parents (Luke 2:51–52). But when His mother came to Him with her concern, Jesus' response shows

He was not willing to be manipulated. He was living according to His heavenly Father's timetable. Jesus knew His place at the centre of His Father's will, acting in obedience to Him and Him only. That is also the most secure place for us to be.

Family relationships change. Growing up, bereavement and separation shape and shake family ties. If your identity is based on these changing foundations, you will never be secure. With your identity secure as God's daughter, you can release those around you, rejoicing when they blossom and find independence; at peace if changes lead to separation.

Christian writer Michele Guinness, herself a Jewish mother, writes: 'When God is the centre of a woman's life, the repository of all her expectations, aspirations and desires, she will no longer need to drain a man [or any other person], or depend on him [or her] for her self-worth.'

Ask yourself some tough questions:
Am I dependent or domineering in my family relationships?
Am I giving life to my family, or draining life?

 Father, Your Son showed His love for You in obedient service. Thank You for the opportunities You give me to demonstrate my love for You by serving others.

No worries

Matthew 6:25–34

'… why do you worry about clothes? … your heavenly Father knows that you need them.' (vv.28,32)

Do you look for security in your appearance? On the TV programme *What Not to Wear*, presenters Trinny and Susannah delight in changing people's appearance, helping them to find new confidence. But, the transformation isn't even skin deep. When the psychological boost wears off, some return to their old ways.

Focusing primarily on what to wear and what to eat distracts us from finding our security in God, who is the source of everything we have.

God used today's reading to speak to me when I was just 12. It was the first time I was ever aware of God underlining a bit of the Bible, just for me. Midi skirts had replaced the mini skirts of the sixties. I wanted one and was sulking. Bizarrely grabbing my Bible as an excuse for keeping the light on later that night, I opened it at Matthew 6 and read: '… why do you worry about clothes? ... seek first his kingdom and his righteousness ...' (vv.28,33).

I was amazed that God knew what I was thinking. He also knew what would be better for me than a new skirt: kingdom priorities. Putting God first; longing for Him and His presence more than anything, is where I find lasting security. He is well able to meet my needs, and has done consistently through more than 40 years.

Security comes from knowing that your loving heavenly Father is the source of everything you need. Outward appearances are fleeting and of no real value. As the much-loved Velveteen Rabbit says: 'Real is a thing that happens to you ... by the time you are Real, most of your hair has been loved off, and your eyes drop out and you get loose in the joints and very shabby.'

 Read Psalm 18, especially verse 19, then give God your needs and worries in exchange for His love and strength.

True riches

Luke 18:18–25

'How hard it is for the rich to enter the kingdom of God!' (v.24)

Today's story reveals how Jesus identified the source of one young man's security. He wanted to have eternal life, but Jesus knew that this rich man's possessions were more important to him than anything else.

Many people – especially those of us living in the affluent West – find security in possessions. We believe the adverts telling us to spend more, acquire more … 'Because you're worth it'. We may secretly covet the Posh and Becks' celebrity lifestyle, believing the lie that more possessions will make us happy.

But, as St Augustine said, 'A person of faith owns the entire wealth of the world, for even though he has almost nothing as his own, if he clings to you, Lord, whom all things serve, he has everything.'

Possessions don't make us rich in eternal terms;

instead, they can get in the way of our relationship with God. It is much more difficult to depend on God, when we can rely on our own resources to meet our daily needs. Often, it is only when we are faced with our own poverty and emptiness that we see God's miraculous provision.

In 1999 in East Timor, near Indonesia, 15,000 people escaping fierce fighting found refuge in the forest around a house run by Sister Lourdes who leads a Christian community. 'We did not have enough food for even 15 people, let alone 15,000,' she says. 'But each day I got up, I prayed, and then I started cooking rice – and the barrel of rice never ran out for three weeks. The day it ran out was the day the international peacekeepers came.'

Our 'liberated' contemporaries want more money, more sex and more power; poverty, chastity and obedience to God may seem restrictive, but they are values which set people free to enjoy God's limitless riches.

 Father God, forgive me when I trust in human resources. You are everything I need.

Living in security

The book of Esther tells the story of a secure woman: an orphan whose beauty catches a king's attention and she becomes queen. Status, clothes, servants – she has it all, but her security does not lie in her appearance or acquired royalty. She trusts in God and risks everything to serve Him and to save her people.

If your weekend offers time to read a good story, these ten chapters in Esther show how a woman lived securely, even when her life was in the balance.

As you read through this guide to personal devotion, use these weekend pages to reflect on and note what God has been saying to you.

Also, if you find yourself thinking about other women who you know would love to experience greater security, pray for them as you pray for yourself.

Then Esther sent this reply to Mordecai: 'Go, gather together all the Jews who are in Susa, and fast for me. Do not eat or drink for three days, night or day. I and my maids will fast as you do. When this is done, I will go to the king, even though it is against the law. And if I perish, I perish.

Esther 4:15–16

My thoughts

Deliver us from evil

Matthew 4:1–11; 6:9–13

'Man does not live on bread alone, but on every word that comes from the mouth of God.' (4:4)

'Compulsive eating can be a lonely and depressing affair in which loving and relying on food can feel safer than loving and relying on people,' writes Helena Wilkinson, who helps people with eating disorders. Alcoholics and drug addicts can have similar reasons for their addiction. But you don't need to be an addict to find security in food, drink or drugs. Comfort eating, numbing senses with an extra glass of wine or popping an extra pill are common substitutes for the security God gives.

Jesus' situation in today's reading isn't the same. He was legitimately hungry after a 40-day fast. But still He resisted Satan's temptation for a quick fix. Jesus only acted on His Father's initiative.

Finding a quick fix for our inner needs is tempting. The longer route of tackling the roots of our insecurity might seem too painful. It might mean finding help from a trained counsellor, or praying through issues with a mature Christian friend.

Jesus taught us to pray: '… lead us not into temptation, but deliver us from the evil one' (Matt. 6:13). We all need to be delivered – or set free – from anything which takes God's place in our lives. Even good things like food can be evil if they stop us finding security in God alone.

Fasting – giving up food for a period of time – is a discipline which has been used by Christians throughout history. It highlights our human weakness and teaches us to keep desires in check. Consider fasting for a day to show yourself the extent to which you rely on food. However, if food is a health issue for you, or you are not 100 per cent fit, ask God for other ways to reveal your sources of security.

 Read 2 Corinthians 1:3–4.
Thank You Father for Your compassion and the comfort You give when I rely on You.

Eternal homemaking

Matthew 6:19–24

'… where your treasure is, there your heart will be also.' (v.21)

Something wasn't quite right about the house when Mum arrived home. Once inside, her suspicions were confirmed. The house had been burgled. Drawers had been emptied, silver cutlery was missing and the ship in a bottle made by Granddad before he drowned at sea had been stolen.

Many people are devastated by burglaries and never quite recover. Mum was calm. The source of her security shone through in the words: 'They are only things. Burglars can't steal what's really valuable.' Mum has spent 70 years storing treasure in heaven.

How might you react in a similar situation? Is your home your castle; your secure place? Is it an expression of your personality, or a source of your identity?

The dust-busting duo Kim and Aggie in the TV series *How Clean is Your House?* show that even drastic action to transform a dirty home, doesn't change hearts. Programmes like *Changing Rooms* have challenged the nation to a frenzy of home make-overs. But fashion soon changes and fabrics fade. The buzz of having a beautiful home can soon give way to 'keeping up with the Jones's'.

It is not easy to buck the acquisitive trend of our society. Millions are spent on advertising every year to make sure we keep spending money on 'treasures' with no lasting value. In fact obsolescence is built in to many of the things we buy; moth and rust still destroy our earthly treasures. Thieves can break in and steal your possessions. If they do, make sure they can't shake your security.

Offering others hospitality or refuge may mean your 'castle' is not as secure as other homes; carpets might be spoilt and crockery broken, but a few carpet stains or a broken mug are a small price to pay when someone's eternal destiny is at stake.

 Father God, please help me to change my focus from short-term goals to see life from Your eternal perspective.

Whitewashed tombs?

Matthew 6:5–13; 23:27–28

'… your Father, who sees what is done in secret, will reward you.' (6:6)

A few years ago my family changed churches. I had been involved in most aspects of our previous church over the years: children's work, homegroups, hospitality, administration … In the new context, I had no 'identity'– no label that would fit me into a role. The change helped me to see how responsibilities can take the place of relationships – especially that crucial relationship with God.

Since starting these meditations, we have been looking at different sources of security – all of which fall short of the security that can be found in knowing God. As you have read the Scriptures and considered where your security lies, perhaps you have found yourself thinking about all the other people you know to whom the notes apply: the neighbour – secure in her ideal home; the colleague

– secure because she's well qualified; the friend
– confident because she always looks immaculate.

You can see where the Scriptures apply to others, but you haven't found that they apply to you. It may be that you've been a Christian for some time. Like me, you have had responsibilities in your church. But watch out: Jesus is at His most blunt when talking to 'religious people' like us.

It can be easy to maintain the external habits and commitments of a godly woman, while becoming hardened to God. This is particularly relevant for people with church responsibilities. When others are looking to you to set a good example, it is easy to lose touch with your own spiritual poverty – or if you are aware of your spiritual need, it is not always easy to find a context where you can be open and honest about your failings.

Find yourself a private time and place, where you can meet with God. Find a more mature Christian who can pray with you and help keep you accountable to God's Word.

 Search me, O God, and guide me (Psa. 139:23–24).

The eyes have it!

Matthew 5:27–30; Song of Songs 4:9–10

'… you have stolen my heart with one glance of your eyes …' (Songs 4:9)

In the classic, clichéd romance, eyes meet across a crowded room and two strangers become caught up in a whirlwind romance. Hollywood suggests that once the whirlwind starts, we can't stop its inevitable course. A lingering glance leads to a harmless coffee together, then a lunch or dinner date … and before you know it passions are aroused which are much more difficult to dampen.

Women in the workplace can be especially vulnerable as light-hearted flirting can seem safe – even fun. Those admiring looks from others can make you feel good. But how can you tell what your affectionate flirting does to those around you? Body language and light-hearted banter can be easily misinterpreted. You may be in control of your feelings, but others might not be so controlled.

Sin slips into our lives subtly. The young bride

might be horrified at the thought of an affair. But ten years and three babies later, an innocent friendship can turn into a romantic fling to boost flagging self-esteem. Satan, the deceiver, always plays dirty. Watch out at those vulnerable times when you are grieving or lonely. Make sure that shoulder-to-cry-on doesn't put you in a compromising situation.

Jesus advocated drastic action to avoid sin. He told His followers that adultery starts with a lingering look – He knows because He knows about the passionate love that captures hearts with a single glance. He feels that passion for us.

Song of Songs is a love story in which the Lover is often interpreted as Jesus. As you read this passionate love poem, imagine Jesus, the Lover, talking to you. He finds your love intoxicating – more so than wine or the best perfume. Invest your emotions in Him. Look to Him for comfort. Ask for His help to guard your heart (Prov. 4:23). Don't get caught looking to others for attention, flattery or appreciation.

 Pour out your love to God – enjoy the security of His love for you.

Closer than a brother

Matthew 16:13–17:8

'What good will it be for a man if he gains the whole world, yet forfeits his soul?' (16:26)

One of the privileges of becoming a Christian is that you join a huge community, drawn from all backgrounds and races, throughout history.

Community is part of God's pattern for living. God is always in community as God the Father, God the Son and God the Holy Spirit. As we become like Him, He wants us to develop close relationships with others. Our tendency in the West to think of ourselves as individuals means sometimes we miss the Bible's community emphasis. As Jesus said, people know we are His followers by the way we love one another (John 13:35). Our unity teaches the world truths about God (John 17:23).

Jesus expects us to be part of the community He calls His Bride, the Church. But occasionally we need to step out of the crowd and stand alone, especially if we are drawing our security from the group rather than God.

In today's Bible reading Peter stands out from the crowd. He knows exactly who Jesus is and is not afraid to say so. This brash, loveable disciple is one of Jesus' closest friends. Peter is with Jesus on the mountain top when Jesus' spiritual identity is revealed and God speaks.

But Jesus has to distance Himself from Peter's well-meaning attempts to divert Him from His destiny. Peter doesn't want Jesus to die. He can't see beyond the short-term feel-good factor he experiences as one of the disciples, to the eternal purposes which take Jesus to the cross.

Do you find security in close friendships? If your security is in your friends you may well be let down – just as Jesus was when Peter betrayed Him. Ask God to show you if your friendships – or your unmet need for friends – have taken the place Jesus should have as the only true source of your security.

 Read Proverbs 18:24. Thank God for Jesus – the friend who sticks by you, whatever happens.

Firm foundations

What props up your security? Career, status, relationships, appearance, possessions, food, drink, your home, church responsibilities, the thrill of romance?

Over the past two weeks we have looked at each of these props, which can take the place of God in our lives. God wants to replace these props to become the only source of your security.

Use this space to list three main areas where you are weakest – the props you turn to most easily when you take your eyes off Jesus.

Read over Song of Songs this weekend. Imagine Jesus is the Lover and you are the Beloved.

Jesus' love is the basis of real security. God wants you to build your life on the firm foundations of that love, so that you can flourish, whatever happens, and however your circumstances change.

Like an apple tree among the trees of the forest is my lover among the young men. I delight to sit in his shade, and his fruit is sweet to my taste. He has taken me to the banqueting hall, and his banner over me is love.

Song of Songs 2:3-4

My thoughts

Knowing God's purpose

Esther 4:14; John 14:1–14

'Do not let your hearts be troubled. Trust in God …'
(John 14:1)

What do Esther and Jesus have in common? Esther is a beautiful Jewish girl, chosen to be queen of a country where all Jews are threatened with death. She turns to God for help, fasting and praying before risking her life to approach the king: '… I will go to the king, even though it is against the law. And if I perish, I perish' she says (Esth. 4:16).

She could have remained silent, but she had a clear sense of purpose. As Mordecai said: '… who knows but that you have come to royal position for such a time as this?' (4:14).

Jesus, our King, chose to set aside the majesty of heaven to rescue us from death and give us eternal life. His clear sense of purpose carries Him through Gethsemane where He prays: 'My Father, if it is possible, may this cup be taken from me. Yet not as I will, but as you will' (Matt. 26:39).

Security like that comes from knowing God's character. When Jesus took our sin upon Himself He was separated from God. But because of His death and resurrection we can know that nothing can separate us from God and His love. It is then that we can dare to follow Him, even to death.

Jesus risked everything for us. He was secure in the knowledge that nothing could happen to Him that was outside God's will – and that ultimately God's plans are for good to triumph.

Perhaps you are facing difficulties or pain that is hard to bear. Perhaps the Bible readings over the past two weeks have highlighted your insecurity or alternative routes to security. During this week we will turn the focus away from ourselves to God, to discover what He is like.

 Jesus puts the responsibility on us: 'Do not let your hearts be troubled.' Bring Him each of your concerns and ask Him to work until good triumphs (Rom. 8:28).

Knowing God's love

John 14:15–31

'He who loves me will be loved by my Father, and I too will love him …' (v.21)

'Spiritual and emotional security comes from having our basic needs met – the need to be loved and to belong, to be valued and feel of worth and to have meaning and purpose in our lives,' says Jeannette Barwick at each of the courses she runs on How to be a Secure Woman.

The first step to security is knowing you are loved.

Adam and Eve, prior to the Fall, could be described as the world's first secure people. They were designed and created by God and maintained a daily relationship with Him, that in turn enabled them to live out their lives in the knowledge that they were loved unconditionally, valued highly, and that every day had point and purpose.

Human love has weaknesses. You might feel you were not really loved as a child; as an adult, circumstances and human failings will mean your experience of being loved is imperfect. You might think that everyone else is loved, except you. But that is simply not true. Every person goes through times when they are uncertain about being loved by the people around them.

Only God's love can be relied on through thick and thin. People who are secure about God's love for them can have confidence through all that life throws at them.

But God's love is not slushy and insubstantial. Jesus makes a clear link between love and obedience: 'If anyone loves me, he will obey my teaching.' Then the promise is certain: 'My Father will love him, and we will come to him and make our home with him' (v.23).

Take comfort from the fact that God loved you, even before you loved Him: '… God demonstrates his own love for us in this: While we were still sinners, Christ died for us' (Rom. 5:8).

Respond to God's initiative by obeying Him, in your relationships, with your money, and in every other aspect of your life.

 Please forgive me when I disobey You or ignore Your guidance. Please give me the strength to live differently.

Knowing I belong

John 15:1–17

'Remain in me, and I will remain in you. No branch can bear fruit by itself …' (v.4)

Fashionable spirituality often focuses on individuals: aromatic oils to make me feel good; crystals to determine my destiny; exercises to empower me … the 'me' focus feeds my selfish consumer instincts. Christianity shifts the focus away from me to God and my community as I learn to love God first, then my neighbour as I love myself.

Christians are part of a worldwide community – Jesus uses the word picture of a vine where we are fruit-bearing branches. And He is committed to producing the best fruit possible in our lives.

If you look back on your journey with God, you might notice times when seemingly good activities have been stopped. A youth group or homegroup you were involved with closed down. Work you were enjoying ended. Friendships changed. With hindsight, can you see how God might have been 'pruning' – changing circumstances to allow you grow stronger or in new directions? The pruning process is sometimes painful, but Jesus is committed to you. Being part of His family means your life will be fruitful.

Security through the difficult pruning processes of life comes from knowing you belong. One of the most special churches I've come across excels in helping people to know they belong. The rest of the world might see some of their members as a motley crew of misfits: unemployed, disabled, ex-drug addicts, people with learning disabilities – but everyone is made to feel special. They belong to Jesus and they belong together. Together they make a difference, bringing love and vitality to their community.

Jesus gives us responsibility again: 'Remain in me …' In other words: make Jesus your secure place. Then you won't have to work at bearing fruit – it is the natural consequence of belonging to Him.

 Are you bearing fruit? Ask God to speak to you about belonging: belonging to Jesus and to your local part of His worldwide family, the Church.

Knowing
I'm valued

John 3:1–21

'For God so loved the world that he gave his one and only Son …' (v.16)

Moses, a young boy in a remote Ugandan village, had a serious accident which left the contents of his abdomen exposed. Without a major operation he would soon die from infection, but a chance meeting with an English Christian woman linked him to a Christian family in the USA who wanted to pay for his treatment.

After the operation, Moses made a full recovery. Months later, the English woman was back in his village and received a visit from Moses' father who wanted to thank her and the American family – not only for his son's life, but because their practical Christian love had changed his life as well as his son's.

Moses' father had been a Muslim but, when his son recovered, he wanted to hear more about the God of love who prompted people he had never met from England and the USA to show such love to his son. So he went to a local church and subsequently became a Christian.

All over the world Christians are demonstrating God's love to neighbours, colleagues and whole communities by showing how every individual matters. Christians value the lives of others because we know how much we are valued by God. Recognising the value of every life prompts Christians to be at the forefront of many healthcare projects, highlighting the value of human life from conception to the grave. No one is worthless.

God considers each one of us to be so valuable that He gave His Son's life to make it possible for us to know Him. The transformation God offers is like being born all over again with a clean slate, fresh hope and the Holy Spirit filling us to overflowing with God's love and life.

 Thank You that I can be secure because You value me, Father God. Your grace means I'm loved, even though I can't do anything to merit Your amazing love.

Knowing the price Christ paid

John 16:17–17:5

'You will grieve, but your grief will turn to joy.' (v.20)

The disciples were sad at the prospect of being separated from Jesus. They didn't understand His purpose for living. Although He was about to die, Jesus' prayer in John 17:1–5 shows He was completely secure. He knows His purpose; He knows He is loved and belongs with His Father; He knows His own value – and He has the satisfaction of knowing He has completed all He has been given to do.

Having chosen this devotional book, you may be aware of some of your insecurities. You may have asked yourself questions like 'Who loves me?' 'Who needs me?' or 'What's the point of my life?' Focusing on Jesus and the security He offers, might have made you feel worse instead of better. Sometimes sadness, uncomfortable feelings or difficult circumstances are God's way of prompting change and growth.

Chinese Pastor Samuel Lamb is known for his quotation, 'Remember the lesson of the Chinese church: more persecution, more growth.' As the pastor explains, 'Before I was put into prison in 1955, this church's membership was 400; when I came out in 1978, it built up to 900 in a matter of weeks. Then after 1990, when everything was confiscated here and the church briefly closed, we re-opened and in a matter of weeks we had 2,000 members. More persecution, more growth – that's the history of the Chinese church, that's the history of this church.'

It is also the story behind most mature Christian lives.

Over the past few weeks perhaps you have faced the hard fact that instead of relying on God, your security lies in your work, relationships, a beautiful body or lavish surroundings … even being spiritual or helping others.

Ask God to forgive you for finding security elsewhere. Ask Him to change your heart and receive the security He offers.

Read Romans 8:31–39.
Thank You Father that nothing can separate me from Your love.

The gratitude attitude

Give God a gift of gratitude. Read Psalm 100 below and put it into practice throughout the weekend.

Whatever you are feeling, God is good. He made you and you are His precious daughter. Write a list of God's characteristics. Use your list as you thank Him and praise Him for His goodness, love and faithfulness through history.

Even if life seems difficult at present, thank God for meeting your most basic needs for food and shelter.

Shout for joy to the LORD, all the earth.
  Worship the LORD with gladness;
  come before him with joyful songs.
Know that the LORD is God.
  It is he who made us, and we are his;
  we are his people, the sheep of his pasture.

Enter his gates with thanksgiving
  and his courts with praise;
  give thanks to him and praise his name.
For the LORD is good and his love endures for ever;
  his faithfulness continues through all
  generations.

My thoughts

I can't make it on my own

Isaiah 53:2–12

'Surely he took up our infirmities and carried our sorrows …' (v.4)

Independence is fashionable – community is an exception not the norm in Western culture, but loneliness is the fruit of our independent ways.

The Wizard of Oz star Judy Garland once said, 'If I'm such a legend, then why am I so lonely? Let me tell you, legends are all very well if you've got somebody around who loves you.' Less than two weeks after her 47th birthday, she was found dead in her bathroom by her fifth husband.

Loneliness has reached epidemic proportions in Britain, and might be related to the fact that the number of one-person households in England and Wales has reached nearly a third of all households.

Independent living may or may not be your choice. Alone, you don't have to adapt to other people's preferences. But, whether you live alone or not, an independent spirit is not godly. It says 'I can make it on my own'.

The first step to becoming secure is to face the fact that you cannot make your life work on your own.

Jesus was despised, rejected – left alone, even by God – but His pain had a purpose. As *The Message* version puts it:

… the fact is, it was our *pains he carried –* our *disfigurements, all the things wrong with* us. *We thought he brought it on himself, that God was punishing him for his own failures. But it was our sins that did that to him, that ripped and tore and crushed him –* our *sins! He took the punishment, and that made us whole. Through his bruises we get healed.*

(vv.4–5)

An independent spirit develops self-protection strategies or ignores the disappointments and hurts which leave us emotionally disabled. Becoming secure means recognising those wounds and receiving the healing that Jesus made available to us at the cross.

 Please Father God, reveal and heal my past hurts, dismantling my self-protection strategies. Help me to rely totally on You.

Fresh start

John 13:1–17; Ephesians 5:25–27

'Unless I wash you, you have no part with me.' (John 13:8)

Jesus is in the beauty business. He is working to prepare a wrinkle-free, blemish-free Bride who is radiant, holy and blameless.

Before any changes take place, He starts by loving us. Think what that means. He loves us when our lives are in a mess; when we are angry, rebellious or wallowing in wrongdoing. He loves us when hurt and disappointment have left us wounded and warped. He loves us when we are cantankerous and disagreeable causing conflict and pain wherever we go.

Jesus wants to give us a fresh start. First we need a bath – that's water baptism when we repent and are made clean. Then He keeps us clean, as Ephesians says, '… to make [us] holy, cleansing [us] by the washing with water through the word …' (v.26).

Jesus said that the 'word is truth' (John 17:17). What might it mean to be washed with truth?

Recently I worked on a project alongside a baroness. She continually praised my stumbling efforts and congratulated every minor accomplishment. In comparison with her world-changing achievements, mine were trivial and insignificant, but her enthusiasm and encouragement made me rise above my normal abilities as I strove to be true to the picture she painted of me. Encouragement is a very special gift.

Jesus sees us, not as we are, but as we will become. He delights in us. When He washes us, He removes the lies we take on board through life and the sin that sticks, returning us to just-bathed cleanliness.

He also sets us an example. He was completely secure in His identity as the all-powerful Son of God, but was willing to kneel at the feet of His disciples doing the work of the lowest servant.

 Have you had the 'bath' that Jesus talked about? Are you letting Him wash you with His words of truth? Are you secure enough in your status as the King's daughter to be humble?

God's initiative

John 5:16–24

'… the Son can do nothing by himself; he can do only what he sees his Father doing …' (v.19)

Did It My Way are the words to a popular karaoke song, and is even played now at funerals – but it is a sad epitaph. Stubborn independence is not God's way to live.

Jesus' attitude on facing death was the complete opposite, shown in His words, 'not my will, but yours'. He had all the power in the universe available to Him, but He only acted on His Father's initiative. He was obedient – even when obedience meant death.

In the 1980s and 1990s the American church pioneer John Wimber encouraged the worldwide Church to follow Jesus' example by asking: 'What is the Father doing?'

He explained: 'We tried to enter each ministry situation with that question foremost in our minds. Our experiences in spiritual gifts were an attempt to discern what the Father was up to. Whether the situation was evangelism, healing, budgeting for the poor, or sending a couple across the country to plant a church, the important thing was to ask the Father what He was doing. To continue to listen is essential because Jesus is still Owner-Occupier of the Church. It is after all, His ministry, His authority, not ours. Our job is to co-operate.'

Take the same approach to your own life. You might have become aware of lots of aspects of your life which need to change. You could try to set your own agenda. But what is God's priority in your life? You are unique and the way God works in and through you is uniquely tailored to fit you – and He might not be in such a hurry as you.

Jesus was surrounded by needy people. How did He choose who to help? He healed many – but there was no formula to the way He healed. He touched some, announced healing to others; He told let others 'your sins are forgiven'.

Jesus was led by the Holy Spirit, just as each of us needs to be.

 Please help me, Father, to learn to follow the Holy Spirit's lead today.

Barren

Matthew 3:13–4:17

'... he saw the Spirit of God descending like a dove and lighting on him.' (v.16)

In the Sahara, globetrotting Michael Palin recognised that the barren and inhospitable desert terrain forces people to look inward for spiritual resources.

On our own we are barren spiritually – just like a desert. We could peel away all the layers of self-protection: the status, achievements, relationships, appearance, possessions ... which have become our security blanket. We could tackle all the wounds which have shaped our character, peeling away the hurts. But we could find that, like an onion, there's nothing left when the layers have gone.

These daily readings may have helped you to recognise areas where you feel alone or barren. But be encouraged. Jesus chose to identify with you. Philippians 2:7 says he 'emptied Himself' (NASB) when he became a man.

Today's Bible reading reminds us that Jesus began His work by receiving the Holy Spirit. As Peter explained: '… God anointed Jesus of Nazareth with the Holy Spirit and power, and … he went around doing good and healing all who were under the power of the devil, because God was with him' (Acts 10:38).

The Holy Spirit is not a vague, feel-good factor. When the Holy Spirit comes, people are transformed: Mary conceived (Luke 1:26–38); Zechariah prophesied (Luke 1:67–80); the disciples received power (Acts 2:1–13); Peter preached – and 3,000 responded (Acts 2:14–41); Stephen was radiant in the face of death (Acts 7:54–60); Saul received his sight (Acts 9:17–19); disciples at Ephesus spoke in tongues and prophesied (Acts 19:1–7); John received his revelation of Jesus Christ and heaven (Rev. 1:1; 4; 21–22).

Jesus went into the desert full of the Holy Spirit. Because He was not alone, He was able to withstand all that the tempter could throw at Him. He lived and worked in the power of the Spirit, and so must we.

 In Acts 19:2 Paul asked some disciples, 'Did you receive the Holy Spirit when you believed?' If you can't respond 'Yes' with confidence, ask a leader in your church to pray with you.

Empowered

Acts 1:4–8

'… you will receive power when the Holy Spirit comes on you; and you will be my witnesses …' (v.8)

Former Communist party worker Soon Ok Lee survived six years of detention in the hell-on-earth conditions of a North Korean prison labour camp. She could not understand how Christians could be the happiest prisoners in the camp, when they were given the worst jobs and worked in the most dangerous areas. Although they were prisoners, they were empowered and strengthened by the Holy Spirit. It was the radiant witness of these suffering believers that led Soon Ok Lee to become a Christian.

'Empowered' is a contemporary buzzword, which can have a militant, rebellious edge, suggesting that those who are empowered will exchange their downtrodden status for new eminence. It does not paint a picture of Jesus' humility and service, quite the opposite.

But Jesus promised to empower us, His disciples. He made a clear distinction between John's water baptism which symbolises repentance, and Holy Spirit baptism which fills His disciples with power. In Acts, when the apostles came across new groups of disciples, they checked that they had been baptised in water and had received the Holy Spirit: washing and filling are both aspects of becoming part of Jesus' family.

A few days ago, we considered how Jesus was baptised in water and received the Holy Spirit, and we saw the impact of the Holy Spirit as people were transformed.

Jesus is still empowering people today. When we are filled with His Spirit, He gives us His authority, His strength and His confidence. But the focus remains on Him, not on experiences or on the gifts the Spirit brings. Being 'witnesses to Jesus' is an automatic consequence of this empowering. That's because we are empowered by the Holy Spirit whose work is to bring glory to Jesus (John 16: 13–14). This empowering makes us humble servants rather than lofty leaders. As we become transparent, Jesus shines through all we do.

 Please Jesus, fill me to overflowing with Your Holy Spirit.

The taste of truth

If you enjoy eating chocolate, you will know how to savour that melting-in-your-mouth moment. But even the most addicted chocoholics enjoy a good meal.

Reading whole books of the Bible at one sitting is like a banquet. If your weekend gives you time and space to read, try reading Ephesians in one sitting, noting any verses God uses to speak particularly to you.

If you are busier at the weekend than in the week, use this page to write your own version of these verses from the first chapter of Ephesians to savour as you get on with the weekend's tasks:

Praise be to the God and Father of our Lord Jesus Christ, who has blessed us in the heavenly realms with every spiritual blessing in Christ. For he chose us in him before the creation of the world to be holy and blameless in his sight.

(vv.3–4)

My thoughts

Receive God's love

Ephesians 1:3–14

'… he chose us in him before the creation of the world to be holy and blameless in his sight.' (v.4)

In the desert after His baptism, the words ringing in Jesus' ears must have been: 'This is my Son, whom I love; with him I am well pleased' (Matt. 3:17). He lived secure in the knowledge that His Father loved Him, until that heart-rending moment on the cross when He cried: 'My God, my God, why have you forsaken me?' (Matt. 27:46). For the only time in eternity, Jesus was separated from His Father. Because of Jesus, we need never know that complete separation from God.

Feeling separated from God and from His love is at the root of all our insecurities. Knowing that God loves you passionately is vital if you are to become more secure.

Paul's teaching is not always easy to read and understand; today's passage from Ephesians is no exception. But it is worth persevering with it because this is a fantastic declaration of all the amazing riches available to us as Christians, who are the objects of God's overwhelming love. Reading it in a variety of Bible versions might help. If you have internet access, use www.biblegateway.com.

God loves you and, as a Christian, every spiritual blessing is available to you; you have been chosen to be holy and blameless; you are part of His long-term adoption plans; His glorious grace (**G**od's **R**iches **A**t **C**hrist's **E**xpense) is freely available to you; He has bought you with Jesus' priceless blood; He forgives your sins; He lavishes you with wisdom and understanding; He makes mysteries known to you; He sees you in Christ when He looks at you; you are marked with the Holy Spirit; you have a guaranteed inheritance.

Being loved by God is the antidote to feeling dirty, impure, shamed, blamed, friendless, worthless, sinful, stupid, excluded or disinherited.

 Over the next week we will be looking at the roadblocks to receiving this amazing love. Ask God for wisdom and He will give it to you (James 1:5).

Risky living

Romans 8:28–39

'Who shall separate us from the love of Christ?' (v.35)

'I won't let myself love wholeheartedly: I've been hurt before; I'll be hurt again.' 'I won't go for promotion: I'm not good enough; I'll feel a failure.' 'I don't expect my life to change: God hasn't got plans for me; I'm nobody special.'

Lies, lies and more lies. What lies do you believe? What lies are you speaking to yourself daily?

Remember that strange concept Jesus talked about: washing with the word – words of truth. This is not the power of positive thinking in action. It's the power of God's truth; His unfailing promises; words waiting to be fleshed out in your life.

What has God promised you? If you don't think He has made you specific promises, use this or previous readings to write yourself a list of God's promises: write how much you are loved, to whom you belong, how much you are valued, what you are worth and what meaning and purpose there is to your life. Make the list specific: 'God promises me …'

God's love and His promises to His people – and to you personally – are building blocks to being secure.

Believing an unseen God might seem like a risky business, which is why we have spent time looking at Jesus and His character. Jesus came to show us what God is like. Knowing God's character helps us to trust His promises and receive His love.

Speak truth to yourself and expect God's words to be fleshed out in you. Wage war on the lies. As Paul said: 'We use our powerful God-tools for smashing warped philosophies, tearing down barriers erected against the truth of God, fitting every loose thought and emotion and impulse into the structure of life shaped by Christ' (2 Cor. 10:5, *Message*).

 Read 1 John 4:13–19. Fear and unbelief block God's love. Admit your fear and unbelief; receive God's forgiveness and revel in His love.

Know God's forgiveness

Psalm 103

'… as far as the east is from the west, so far has he removed our transgressions from us.' (v.12)

When Bishop Festo Kivengere was given permission to talk to three men before they were executed under the brutal rule of Idi Amin in Uganda, he thought 'How do you give the gospel to doomed men who are probably seething with rage?'

He approached the trio, who were standing in chains before the firing squad.

Before he could say anything, one of the men burst out: 'Bishop, thank you for coming! I wanted to tell you, the day I was arrested, in my prison cell, I asked the Lord Jesus to come into my heart. He came in and forgave me all my sins! Heaven is now open, and there is nothing between me and my God! Please tell my wife and children that I am going to be with Jesus. Ask them to accept Him into their lives as I did.' The other two men told similar stories, excitedly raising their hands, which rattled their handcuffs.

As the Bishop translated what the men said, the soldiers were so astonished that they forgot to put hoods over the men's faces! The three faced the firing squad standing close together. They looked towards the people and began to wave, handcuffs and all. The people waved back. Then the fatal shots were fired …

The security those men knew in the face of death, came from a clear encounter with God and the certainty that they were forgiven and belonged to Jesus. Although they had only been Christians for a short time, they knew death could not separate them from Him. They were free from guilt.

Genuine guilt and feelings of guilt can be a roadblock to security. Ask God to show you if you need to ask His forgiveness for rebellious attitudes or anything you have said or done.

 Read 2 Corinthians 7:10 and 1 John 1:9. Confess past sins to God, then ask for His help to keep a clean slate.

Forgiving others

Matthew 18:21–35

'The servant's master took pity on him, cancelled the debt and let him go.' (v.27)

'I've got to forgive them. I still forgive them. My family and I still stand by what we believe: forgiveness.'

This was the reaction of Anthony Walker's mother, Gee, to her son's murderers. Anthony was killed with a mountaineering axe, simply because he was black. After sitting through the two-week trial at Liverpool Crown Court, Gee said: 'Do I forgive them? At the point of death Jesus said "I forgive them because they don't know what they did." I've got to forgive them …'

In the same year, Abigail Witchalls was left paralysed after a knife attack. When Richard Cazaly, the prime suspect in the case, committed suicide, Abigail's mother said: 'His death is the real tragedy in this story because he lost his life …'

When *Crimewatch* presenter Fiona Bruce

interviewed Abigail's husband Benoit, she said, 'It is remarkable that you can talk in such a forgiving and tolerant way about someone who has done something so terrible to your family.'

Forgiveness sets people free. The Walkers and the Witchalls will still have to cope with pain, grief and many other difficulties, but they have not allowed evil to make them bitter or hard-hearted.

Most of us do not have to face such traumas, but we are all wronged at sometime and need to forgive those who offend, ill-treat or wound us. Unforgiveness acts like a dam, blocking the flow of God's love and grace in our lives. When we refuse to forgive others, we are the ones who lose out.

Spend some time thinking about the different groups of people you know or have known, asking God to show you if you are harbouring unforgiveness towards anyone. Some will be part of your past, others might be people you see regularly.

Forgiveness is not a feeling, it is a conscious decision before God.

 Father, as I forgive _____ , please show me if I need to put forgiveness into words.

Trusting God

Psalm 25

'To you, O Lᴏʀᴅ, I lift up my soul; in you I trust … Do not let me be put to shame …' (vv.1–2)

An MRI scan revealed that Kerry Southey had a secondary cancerous tumour pressing on her spine. On the same day as the scan, the oncologists put her in for the first of nine radiation treatments on the tumour.

'We are all gutted!!' she wrote in a newsletter to friends and supporters of her ministry based in South Africa, as she explained her family's reaction. 'Without the Lord we'd hate to walk this path, but we're valuing each day to the full despite the situation. Knowing that in Jesus we'll have eternity together makes a big difference – but it is SO painful!!'

Kerry is honest about how she feels: 'I fight fear of the process of death and wage war on thoughts of the ugliness and pain of such things. I have the sudden waves of abject exhaustion that occasionally hit me and make me feel like someone pulled the bathplug of my life and it's draining away. Then I have to grab back on to Jesus with all my frail strength and say "It's about You Jesus – Your power, Your glory, Your love and Your holding my life in Your hands."'

Almost everyone reading this will know someone with cancer. Our response at these most difficult times in life shows where our security lies. God is committed to us, especially through difficult times, showing us how to rely on Him.

This psalm is the prayer of a man in trouble. Its three themes of forgiveness, guidance and protection are repeated throughout the psalm, which has one line for each letter of the Hebrew alphabet rather than developing a logical argument.

Are you able to trust God to take care of your life, whatever happens?

 Write out the lines from this psalm that seem most relevant to your situation. Use them as a prayer, declaring your trust in God to forgive, guide and protect you in every situation.

A transformed life

Bereavement, a bitter mother-in-law, life as a foreigner in a strange land facing food shortages and poverty: Ruth's life included more difficulties than most of us have to face. But she chose to follow God. Read her story in the Bible book of Ruth, to discover how her life was transformed.

Describe the roadblocks you are facing on your journey with Jesus. These might include self-protection: 'I won't trust God – I'll develop my own strategies for living'; unforgiveness: 'I can't let go of the hurts I've received'; unbelief: 'I can't change'; childish petulance: 'I want my own way and if I can't have it I'm not changing!'; unwillingness to take responsibility for your own spiritual state: 'It's all very difficult; I still need someone else to spoon-feed me my spiritual food' or complacency: 'I'm not so bad.'

What does the Bible have to say about the difficulties you face? The following verses may prove helpful: Proverbs 3:5–6; Matthew 6:12–15; Mark 9:14–29; Hebrews 12:2–4; 1 Corinthians 13:11; Philippians 3:7–14.

My thoughts

Getting ready for change

Deuteronomy 1; Romans 12:1–2

'… be transformed by the renewing of your mind.'
(Rom. 12:2)

When the Israelites were on their way to the promised land they set up camp and began to settle, but God said: 'You have stayed long enough … Break camp …' (Deut. 1:6).

He is saying the same to you now. You have been insecure long enough. Get ready to change.

God reminded the people that He had given them the land to possess: 'Do not be afraid; do not be discouraged' (v.21), He said. But the Israelites focused on giants in the land, rather than God's strength. They refused to move (v.28).

What are the 'giants' which stop you being secure in God?

As I began to consider the giants in my own life which stop me moving forward, it was as if God said to me: 'Come on Catherine. What are you waiting for? As a teenager you started out on an adventure with me, but all through your twenties you bleated on about being single. I had the perfect man in mind for you, but were you content to wait? Oh no … you went through agonies and you didn't have to. My plans for you are perfect. Then in your thirties you struggled against the brain-dead years of being a new mum: "Look at how messy my life is" was the thought that paralysed you. In your forties and it's: "I need to be more qualified." What are you waiting for? Your pension? Then you'll be too worried about your health to act on My promises.'

What is God saying about the giants in your life? Has God given you promises which you refuse to believe? What excuses do you make? It is time to move forward.

Security starts with a belief not a feeling: believing that God loves you, values you and has plans for you.

 Thank You Father for Your promises to me. Please give me Your strength to be a 'giant-killer'.

Testing and perseverance

James 1:2–18

'Perseverance must finish its work so that you may be mature and complete, not lacking anything.' (v.4)

'Not lacking anything.' If it is true that the mature, complete 'me' will lack *nothing* – then each of those issues we considered in the first two weeks of these notes, will be taken care of: career, achievement, status, family relationships, appearance, money and possessions, food and drink, my home, friendships and responsibilities.

The challenges I face on the way – the giants – are to develop my spiritual muscles.

It is as if God is saying: 'Of course there are giants; you're not tourists in the land. You are part of an army, commissioned to go in and possess what I have promised to give you. Yes, there will be giants, and you will face opposition. People won't always like you. You'll face hardship and difficulty. It goes with the territory. But you are not grasshoppers, you are giant-killers. You are strong, because I am strong.

You can have courage, because of the promises I have given you; promises for you, your family and for your church family. I will do all I have promised.'

So what about those giants? When I think about the giants which stop me advancing, depression is the biggest giant. Just when I seem to be making headway I feel vulnerable, tearful. But God has been helping me to tackle that giant. Some people need medical help with depression. Others need to get more exercise and better sleep, or to avoid the stresses which start the downward spiral. If depression is a giant in your life, find help. Tackle the giant.

Your giants might be loneliness, financial worries or relationships. Start believing that God is able to make you complete – lacking nothing. Find a Christian friend to pray with regularly, to tackle the giants which hinder you.

 God's says: 'My grace is sufficient for you, for my power is made perfect in weakness' (2 Cor. 12:9).
Please God, give me your grace and strength to defeat those giants.

A woman of purpose

Esther 4:5–7:10

'… who knows but that you have come to royal position for such a time as this?' (4:14)

'Mirror, mirror on the wall, who is the fairest of them all?' In King Xerxes' reign, the answer was an orphan called Esther. She won the king's favour and was crowned queen.

Esther was wise as well as beautiful, but humble enough to take advice. When her people, the Jews, were threatened with death, her uncle challenged her to act. Esther knew she might die as a result of her action, but she risked her life to save her people.

She didn't rely on her beauty or status. She relied on God and made careful plans, fasting and praying as she prepared to petition the king.

On the crucial night, the king couldn't sleep and asked for the national records to be read to him. By 'chance' he discovered that Esther's uncle had not been rewarded for his loyal service. As a result the tables were turned on the man who had planned to kill Esther's uncle and all of the Jews.

Queen Esther was concerned about others rather than herself and was willing to act, even though it put her own life in danger. Being an orphan and being one of the rejected race of Jews, did not hinder Esther; instead those facts played a vital part in God's plan. She was secure in the knowledge that God was in control. As a result of her purposeful action, Esther and her people were saved.

Has God put you into a situation where He can use you? God seems to delight in weaving all the varied experiences of our lives into His wonderful plans. Our lives are like a tapestry. From one perspective they can look like a mess of unconnected threads. But, in reality, those threads make up a beautiful, unique design.

Ask God to reveal His perspective on your life.

Read Romans 8:28.
Father, please show me what You are using for good in my life as You help me to become secure.

A woman covered with love

Ruth 1; 3

'Where you go I will go … Your people will be my people and your God my God.' (1:16)

We saw yesterday that Esther's beauty and status did not replace the security she had in God. God can use all the gifts He gives us as part of His plans.

Today we see how God meets a woman's basic needs for food and relationships. In the ten years before she was widowed, Ruth must have seen enough of God in her in-laws to want their God to be her God. When it comes to a choice between the home and family she knows, and a foreign country which had no food in time of famine, Ruth chooses the bleaker option: vulnerability and poverty with a bitter mother-in-law and without the prospect of a husband. Perhaps she already realises that life with God is always the best choice, however bleak it might seem.

Naomi is adamant: '… the LORD's hand has

gone out against me!' (1:13). She doesn't seem to acknowledge that God has provided Ruth to meet her needs, though by the end of the story (4:16) she is the picture of contentment and, later, the Saviour of the world traces His family tree back to her grandson (Matt. 1:5).

Ruth is loyal and hard-working. Her faithful, kind character catches the attention of Boaz, who becomes the answer to his own prayer (2:12).

Notice the parallel between Boaz and Ruth's romance and our relationship with Jesus. Jesus is our 'kinsman-redeemer' who pays a ransom to restore us to a right relationship with God. He covers us with 'robes of righteousness' (Isa. 61:10) – our messy lives are covered with His royal perfection.

Some women's response to vulnerability can be to become hard or handicapped. Ruth takes neither route. She knows that she needs to be covered, protected and loved. It is important to know your weaknesses – but vital to rely on God, not your own devices to find strength.

 Father God, please help me to rely on You. Thank You for covering me with Your love and protection.

A woman who saw Jesus

John 20:1–18

'Mary Magdalene went to the disciples with the news: "I have seen the Lord!"' (v.18)

Mary Magdalene's life was transformed because she met Jesus: Mark tells us that Jesus delivered her from seven demons (16:9). There's no indication of what she was like in her possessed state – but she must have been a messed-up lady.

The Mary Magdalene we meet in the Gospels is passionate in her love for Jesus. Her life is an expression of gratitude to the One who set her free. She is in the forefront of the action, faithful at the foot of the cross when most of Jesus' followers deserted Him; first to tell the disciples that the stone had been rolled away from the tomb's entrance; and first to meet the risen Lord.

She does not seem to be embarrassed to show emotion. She's probably not the woman who anointed Jesus' feet and wiped them with her hair

(John 12: 1–10) – but it's the type of extravagant, impulsive gesture we might expect from her.

Meeting Jesus transforms lives. Giving yourself wholeheartedly to Him, responding with gratitude to His love and seeking to put Him first, will shift the whole focus of your life. As you move forward with God, it is vital to learn to speak truth not lies to yourself, concentrating on facts not feelings, tackling the 'giants' which undermine your security.

Sometimes, like Mary Magdalene, you might need extra help. After a miscarriage, I found help from a Christian counsellor as I came to terms with losing a baby. If you do need spiritual or emotional help, make sure the person you approach is accountable to others and working within clear guidelines on personal conduct, confidentiality and competence. And don't look to that other person for the security you are lacking, look to Jesus – although He might use the other person as He sets you free.

 Emotions are part of God's special gift to you as a woman. Don't be afraid to show emotion as you respond to Jesus' love.

Rest and
be thankful

The book of Hebrews provides keys which unpack the whole of the Bible. It explains who Jesus is in the context of Jewish history.

The writer points us to 'Sabbath-rest' – the complete security, joy and satisfaction which God has promised us in Christ.

Although Hebrews was written to encourage Jews who became Christians, it urges all believers to become mature. It shows how Old Testament practices of covenant, sacrifice and priesthood are fleshed out in Jesus and the Church.

Try reading it through at one sitting – or at least Hebrews 1:1–4; 3:1–14; 4:14–6:12 and 9:1–10:25, noting any new thoughts which occur to you about Jesus as you read.

Once you have completed these devotions on being secure, you might like to study Hebrews in more depth, to gain an insight into the big picture of God's rescue plan for human history. Reading a Bible book from beginning to end means you can't avoid the verses God wants to use to challenge you.

My thoughts

CWR produce many resources to help you with
regular Bible study. Visit their website at
www.cwr.org.uk.

Believing and becoming secure

Hebrews 10:19–25; 11:1

'Now faith is being sure of what we hope for and certain of what we do not see.' (11:1)

Two months ago I planted three hyacinth bulbs in a pot, watered them and left them in the dark. Today, their strong perfume distracts me as I write; their fleshy pink flower-heads are large and strong; they remind me that winter will soon be over. They prompt the question: how did such beauty emerge from such wizened drabness?

It was the beauty of creation which confronted the author C.S. Lewis's atheism, again and again, until he could no longer deny God's existence. Describing the night he became a Christian, Lewis wrote: 'Total surrender, the absolute leap in the dark, were demanded. I gave in, and admitted that God was God … perhaps, that night, the most dejected and reluctant convert in all England.'

Before becoming a Christian Lewis had no hope: he was like a man in his imaginary world of Narnia, where it was 'always winter, never Christmas'. Faith gave him hope. The joy of knowing God surprised him.

CWR's founder Selwyn Hughes often said: 'Faith sees the invisible, believes the incredible and receives the impossible!' You may not think you have much faith, but God, who is in you because the Holy Spirit lives in you – He is the faithful One, as today's reading reminds us.

The truths you have been considering through these meditations are like bulbs. Given the right conditions, they will flower. Because of all Jesus has done in your life, you can be confident as you approach God. You can be secure, if your security rests on God, the unshakable, faithful One.

Write down ways in which God has been faithful to you.

 During this week we will be using the prayer Jesus taught His disciples. Today, put the first part of that prayer into your own words: 'Our Father in heaven, hallowed be your name …' (Matt. 6:9). ('Hallowed' means to set apart as holy; to respect or honour greatly.)

Seeing the invisible

Hebrews 12:1–6

'Let us fix our eyes on Jesus, the author and perfecter of our faith …' (v.2)

I n Hans Christian Andersen's story, *The Snow Queen*, Gerda finally reaches the icy country where the Snow Queen has taken her friend Kay. Confronted with the wicked queen's guards, she begins to pray the Lord's Prayer. As she prays, angels appear around her with helmets on their heads, carrying shields and spears. The Snow Queen's troops are defeated and Gerda fearlessly enters the palace protected and unhurt.

Paul acknowledges that there are 'spiritual forces of evil in the heavenly realms' (Eph. 6:12) but he reminds the Ephesians: '… be strong in the Lord and in his mighty power. Put on the full armour of God so that you can take your stand against the devil's schemes' (Eph. 6:10–11).

Our focus should always be on Jesus who has defeated the opposition and equips us to stand secure in His love.

Like runners in a marathon, we fix our eyes on the finishing line where we will meet Jesus face to face. But you don't become a marathon runner only by thinking or reading about the prize. You must prepare: put on the running shoes; shed the extra layers of clothing … and then you must begin to run.

Similarly you don't become a secure woman only by thinking about Jesus and wanting to be secure. You need to act, believing that, as you step out, you will be secure.

Martin Luther King said, 'I have a dream … I have a dream that my four little children will one day live in a nation where they will not be judged by the color of their skin but by the content of their character … I have a *dream* today!'

What's your dream? As a totally secure woman, what will you be like? Write yourself a job description and bring it to God as you pray:

Father, '… your kingdom come, your will be done on earth as it is in heaven …' in my life and in those around me.

Believing the incredible

2 Peter 1:3–11

'His divine power has given us everything we need for life and godliness …' (v.3)

In Archbishop Desmond Tutu's book *God Has a Dream* (Doubleday, 2004) he writes: 'During the darkest days of apartheid I used to say to P.W. Botha, the president of South Africa, that we had already won, and I invited him and other white South Africans to join the winning side. All the "objective" facts were against us – the pass laws, the imprisonments, the teargassing, the massacres, the murder of political activists – but my confidence was not in the present circumstances but in the laws of God's universe.'

Tutu recognises God's unchangeable character; His justice which means there is no way that evil, injustice, oppression and lies can have the last word. Despite all the evidence that seems to be to the contrary, God is in charge.

He adds: 'Many of us can acknowledge that God

cares about the world but can't imagine that God would care about you or me individually. But our God marvelously, miraculously cares about each and every one of us. The Bible has this incredible image of you, of me, of all of us, each one, held as something precious, fragile in the palms of God's hands. And that you and I exist only because God is forever blowing God's breath into our being. And so God says to you, "I love you. You are precious in your fragility and your vulnerability. Your being is a gift. I breathe into you and hold you as something precious.'"

God invites you to take on His divine nature as you become a secure woman. A secure woman is faithful and good; she has wisdom and self-control; perseverance and godliness; she is known for her kindness and love. These are qualities which God's Holy Spirit produces in us (Gal. 5:22).

Bring your needs to Him today as you allow Him to fill you to overflowing with His Spirit.

 'Give us today our daily bread' (Matt. 6:11).

Receiving the impossible

Luke 6:27–38

'Forgive, and you will be forgiven … with the measure you use, it will be measured to you.' (vv.37–38)

Incarcerated in Ravensbruck concentration camp, Betsie ten Boom told her sister Corrie: 'God will give us the love to be able to forgive our enemies.' Corrie wasn't so sure. Betsie died in Ravensbruck on 16 December 1944, but Corrie was released. At the age of 53, she began a worldwide ministry which took her into more than 60 countries in the next 33 years.

Although Corrie had vowed never to return to Germany, she was invited back on a speaking engagement. Her first talk was on forgiveness, and as she was speaking, she saw one of her former prison guards sitting in the audience. At the end of her talk he approached her with a beaming smile, 'How grateful I am for your message Frauline. To think that, as you say, he has washed my sins away!' Taking his outstretched hand, says Corrie, was the hardest thing she had ever had to do in her life. But, as she did so, she found Bestie's words were true: 'The hate in my heart was absorbed and gone,' Corrie said.

Humanly speaking it seemed impossible to forgive a man who had been part of the regime which was responsible for the deaths of so many of Corrie's family, friends and fellow countrymen. But faith in God enables us to receive the impossible: in Corrie's case, the grace to forgive. She didn't feel like forgiving him, but she acted in a forgiving way, reaching out to take his hand, before discovering that God had worked His miracle of grace.

You may *feel* no different from when you first started these devotions, but set your feelings aside. Instead, act on the fact that God has forgiven you; He loves you; He is unshakable.

 Do not let unforgiveness hinder your relationship with God. Ask God for the grace to pray honestly and sincerely: 'Forgive us for doing wrong, as we forgive others' (Matt. 6:12, CEV).

Expect opposition

2 Timothy 3

'All Scripture is God-breathed and is useful for teaching, rebuking, correcting and training …' (v.16)

It is possible to reach this point in this book and to have recognised your false sources of security; to have focused on Jesus to discover the foundation for a secure life; to have faced the fact that you can't make it on your own; and to have considered the issues which block you from becoming a secure woman … and yet you are not ready to move forward.

Ask yourself, 'Am I like one of these "weak-willed women … always learning but never able to acknowledge the truth"?'

It is possible to read the truth about God and His unshakable character; to be told that He loves you and has good plans for you; to hear about how the power of the Holy Spirit is available to transform your life … and to deny God's power, rejecting His truth.

If you identify with that description, then you are

not ready to move on to next week's meditations. Instead, read from Ephesians every day for the next week, asking God to make His truth come alive to you.

Some people think that faith is a crutch, but as we have seen, the opposite is true. We use many different crutches in life to prop up our flagging security. Being a Christian can be tough going, as Paul reminds Timothy in today's reading. Paul says we will face opposition if we want to live godly lives. That's when it is crucial to know the truth about God.

When Jesus faced temptation, He responded to Satan's taunts by quoting Scripture. You need to know what the Bible says to use it in your defence. Knowing the Bible is vital if you are to remain secure. Use tapes or CDs of the Bible, or Scripture set to music, if it suits your learning style better than books.

 '... lead us not into temptation, but deliver us from the evil one' (Matt. 6:13).

Willing and
ready to go?

If you are still not willing to move forward, take a break from these meditations until you have read Ephesians right through, looking out for truths about God and truths about what it means to be 'in Christ'.

Notice, I didn't ask if you were 'ready' or 'able' to move forward. You will never feel ready or able, it is an act of your will: 'I *will* believe that God is good; His plans for me are good; His discipline in my life does me good; His Holy Spirit equips me for good …'

In Paul's words from Ephesians 3:14–21, my prayer for you, and for all those reading these studies is:

… I kneel before the Father, from whom his whole family in heaven and on earth derives its name. I pray that out of his glorious riches he may strengthen you with power through his Spirit in your inner being, so that Christ may dwell in your hearts through faith. And I pray that you, being rooted and established in love, may have power, together with all the saints, to grasp how wide and

long and high and deep is the love of Christ, and to know this love that surpasses knowledge – that you may be filled to the measure of all the fulness of God.

Now to him who is able to do immeasurably more than all we ask or imagine, according to his power that is at work within us, to him be glory in the church and in Christ Jesus throughout all generations, for ever and ever! Amen.

If you are willing to move forward as a secure woman, rooted in God's love for you and drawing on His power to equip you, read John 19 and 20, plus Acts 1:1–9 over the weekend. Write yourself a reminder of what your security cost, and what God promises you as a result of Jesus' suffering, death and resurrection.

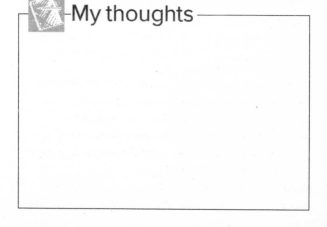

My thoughts

Secure and straightforward

1 Peter 2:1–5, 9–17; 3:1–9

'… you are a chosen people, a royal priesthood, a holy nation, a people belonging to God …' (2:9)

What is a secure woman like? As Peter emphasises, you are secure because God has chosen you. Your role as part of a 'royal priesthood' means you have a purpose in the way you relate to God and to other people.

Just as priests in the Old Testament Temple brought sacrifices and offerings to God, our task as Christians is to bring sacrifices of praise to God, offering our lives to Him daily. Also, just as the priests moved between the outer and inner courts of the Temple, we show the rest of the world what God is like. When Moses had been in the presence of God, his face shone. Being in God's presence will transform your life too.

The whole of the priest's life was dedicated to serving God and His people. That purpose dictated everything the priest did; any practices which might make them unclean and unable to enter God's presence were avoided. The same goes for us today.

Priests serve others, just as Jesus humbled Himself and served. The subject of submission is an issue which has been obscured by controversy in today's Church. But submission is a priestly attitude which enables us to serve others as Jesus did. Job titles are a red herring. All Christians are called to be part of God's holy priesthood, working with God as He builds us together.

Sometimes we women can be like enemies in the camp. Instead of exercising the priestly role of serving and blessing, we use words to destroy instead of building up. We undermine others with our subtle opposition, reminding them of their weaknesses and failings. We criticise their every move. We don't allow them to fail.

Secure women are straightforward in their relationships with others; not manipulating, but life-giving.

 Father, please show me how to exercise the role You have given me as part of Your royal priesthood.
Read James 1:26 and ask for God's help to use words positively.

Accept others

Romans 12:3–21

'… in Christ we who are many form one body, and each member belongs to all the others.' (v.5)

Have you realised that your body is a visual aid to show you spiritual truths? When God made man and woman He made us in His image. We are all God's image-bearers.

The Church, the Body of Christ, also reveals what God is like. Paul describes the Church, here and in 1 Corinthians 12, as a body where everyone has a vital part to play.

As you've been thinking about being a secure woman, you might have thought: 'I want to be like her, not like me!' You recognise attributes in others which you would like to develop in yourself, but remember, God has made you unique, with a unique part to play in His Body.

For example, you might wish you were less emotional. Certainly, God might want to help you to be more self-controlled. Self-control is a fruit of His

Holy Spirit. But don't despise your emotions. Our world needs those who weep with those who weep, as well as people who are good at rejoicing and celebrating others' successes.

When my ten-year-old son's football team is praised and encouraged, they grow noticeably stronger. Even the weakest team members feel they are playing an important part. Faced with a barrage of criticism, they shrivel up and start blaming each other for their failure.

Are you an encourager or a critic? Perhaps you can see faults in others and find yourself wanting to change them. In marriage, how many wives think 'I'll change my husband' and we harp on about their faults and failings? Cynthia Heald's definition of submission in marriage is: 'Ducking low enough so God can touch your husband.' Instead of demanding change in others, recognise their unique qualities and learn to affirm their strengths, rather than highlighting their weaknesses.

 Lord, please help me to love others and to see their qualities as You see them ... and please change me.

Know yourself

Titus 3:3–11

'… he saved us, not because of righteous things we had done, but because of his mercy.' (v.5)

Pantomime-goers know that even the most beautiful ball gowns can't make Cinderella's sisters attractive. They are malicious, envious and hateful. If only they could see themselves as others see them.

We might like to think of ourselves as Cinderella rather than one of her sisters: inner beauty waiting to be recognised and clothed in royal robes. In fact, we are like the ugly sisters. There's nothing attractive about us before God rescues us, washes us clean and renews us by His Spirit. But then, He makes us His heirs; full of hope; equipped by His Spirit to do good.

Do you behave like an ugly sister, like Cinderella in the ashes, or like the chosen princess? Do you remain the same person whoever you are with, or are you a chameleon, changing yourself by putting on airs and graces with some people, and a subservient attitude with others?

Learn to understand your own body language. If you are a chameleon, ask God to help you become more secure as the daughter of the King of kings. A secure woman knows her weaknesses and draws on God's strength. She does not always need to be liked, but is secure knowing that her heavenly Father always loves her even when she makes mistakes. She doesn't crumple under criticism, but can ask, 'Is there something God wants me to learn from this; do I need to change?'

We all have distracting mannerisms and annoying habits. As a secure woman, you can ask a close friend to be honest with you about your mannerisms and habits – not because you should change to please others, but to help you to be gracious with others and improve relationships.

And sometimes you need to be kind to yourself. Secure women know when to rest and find new strength.

 **Because You care for me, I lack nothing I need. Thank You, Father.
Read Psalm 23.**

Know your enemy

1 Peter 5:5–11

'… the devil prowls around like a roaring lion looking for someone to devour. Resist him …' (vv.8–9)

Ezekiel was a priest, but he was living in exile in Babylon, miles away from the Temple. Circumstances meant he couldn't exercise the ministry he had trained for, but God gave him a new ministry to fit those new circumstances. He became a prophet, sent to speak to God's obstinate, stubborn people.

Women often have to adapt to changing circumstances: maybe you thought you'd have a career – but now you have to care for ailing parents or small children. You thought you'd live 'happily ever after' – but now you're disabled or you've been made redundant. You thought marriage was for life – but you're suddenly single again.

God is not limited by your circumstances. He may have different plans for you in the different seasons of your life.

A challenge on the road to security is to remain humble, relying on God in all situations. It is easy to become complacent when life is going well, or anxious when life is difficult. Secure women may be hurting or disappointed but will look to God for His grace and strength. They are self-controlled and alert in good and bad times.

Recognise the times and areas when and where you are vulnerable. Satan is always ready to plant seeds of bitterness or unforgiveness when you least expect it. Avoid arguments late at night when you are tired and likely to go to sleep angry, for example. Don't tackle difficult issues when you're pre-menstrual and know it will end in tears. Don't watch a slushy romance on TV when you're feeling lonely or unloved.

In their seminar on Pioneering Marriage, church leaders David and Philippa Stroud say they head for a coffee shop if they expect a discussion might become over-heated. For them, discussing difficult issues in a public context keeps a rein on angry words.

As a secure woman, learn to recognise and resist Satan's subtle strategies to pull you down.

 May the God of all grace, who called you … make you strong, firm and steadfast.

Focus on Jesus

Colossians 3:1–17

'Since, then, you have been raised with Christ, set your hearts on things above …' (v.1)

Mrs Yang is 73 years old and the survivor of ten years in a Chinese labour camp. How did she survive? She told a staff member from the persecution charity Open Doors, that singing is her secret. If she goes 20 sentences without breaking into song, it is unusual.

Mrs Yang explains, 'We must sing to keep up the spirit – that is how we look up to God, and how we gird up our frame to follow Him.' Then she bursts into song, singing with a cracked contralto, her face full of expression, fists clenched with emphasis and punching the air with the beat.

When Mrs Yang sits down to a meal, she sings a hymn. When she reads her Bible, she starts and finishes with a hymn. When she was locked into a cell with no light, she sang hymns.

Try this habit of holiness. Sing to God by yourself,

says Mrs Yang: 'Singing a hymn forces your whole person to focus on God, to move into an attitude of thankfulness again. The fastest way to realise your life is full of the grace of God is to sing reminders to yourself.'

Women who are secure in God are not focused on themselves and their own circumstances, but on Jesus and all He promises for us – now and in eternity. The old, insecure woman has died. The new woman knows she is chosen, holy and dearly loved. Each day, whether in a prison camp or a suburban semi, she dresses in the royal robes Christ gives her; clothes of compassion, humility, gentleness and patience which show the world the qualities and character she has come to know in her Saviour, Jesus. She knows she has been forgiven, so forgives others. Love flows out of her and unites her with Christians from all backgrounds and circumstances, as they work together doing their world good.

 Make Jude 24 and 25 your prayer.

Complete in Him

Having completed these devotional notes, you will know that the journey with God is not always easy, but you can rest and be secure in Him. Your adventure with Him is still only beginning. He loves you passionately and has your best interests at heart.

Keep your eyes focused on Jesus. Give yourself to worshipping Him wholeheartedly. Keep yourself open to God by reading the Bible and being refreshed daily by the Holy Spirit. Keep yourself teachable, by asking others to pray with you regularly and to remind you of God's truth when you are tempted to believe lies. And remember: '... God who started this great work in you ... [will] bring it to a flourishing finish on the very day Christ Jesus appears (Phil. 1:6, *The Message*).

So this is my prayer: that your love will flourish and that you will not only love much but well. Learn to love appropriately. You need to use your head and test your feelings so that your love is sincere and intelligent, not sentimental gush. Live a lover's life, circumspect and exemplary, a life Jesus will be proud of: bountiful in fruits from the soul, making Jesus Christ attractive to all, getting everyone involved in the glory and praise of God.

(Phil. 1:9–11, *The Message*)

My thoughts

'This teaching changed my life ...'

The How to be a Secure Woman (HTBASW) teaching has impacted the lives of thousands of women through seminars and the workbook – here are just a few of their testimonies:

In April 2005 I attended the HTBASW seminar. The focus was Esther, and her faithfulness, courage and honesty inspired me. A month later my own faith, security and courage were to be sorely tried, when my beloved husband died suddenly.

Nothing could have prepared me for that awful event and yet I experienced God's grace, love and compassion, in amazing ways. I became keenly aware that God was bringing to mind so much of what had been shared at the seminar and He was sustaining me just as He had Esther – 'for such a time as this'!

Jesus is more real, more precious, and I know that in Him I am a secure woman!

Sandra Norgate,
local organiser of seminar in Buckingham

I am part of a dynamic small group called Sister Act which recently headed off for a family-free weekend of fun and fellowship including three sessions based on the *HTBASW* booklet. We were all challenged on different levels about where our securities lay … and spent many hours poring over Bible passages speaking of God's delight in us and discussing what those truths mean for each of us. Many were able to pray out loud and take communion for the first time ever in their Christian walk. Lots of tears and laughter marked the weekend and we're already saving for a repeat performance.

Lisa Phillips,
Crawley Baptist Church

A friend had just experienced flooding in her home and the fear of the floodwaters returning was huge. She was left feeling depressed and insecure, wondering if God really did love her in the same way as she knew He loved others. We committed to journey through the *HTBASW Workbook* together and rediscovered just how special we each are to God, how He has a purpose for each one of us and is interested in every aspect of our lives – even when it seems that God is far away, He is at work in our lives in ways beyond our imagination.

Listening to my friend addressing Christian women in our church recently, I couldn't help asking myself, 'A more secure woman?' Absolutely!

Sandra Taylor,
Pastoral Assistant, All Saints Church, Laleham

National Distributors

UK: (and countries not listed below)
CWR, Waverley Abbey House, Waverley Lane, Farnham, Surrey GU9 8EP.
Tel: (01252) 784700 Outside UK +44 1252 784700

AUSTRALIA: CMC Australasia, PO Box 519, Belmont, Victoria 3216.
Tel: (03) 5241 3288 Fax: (03) 5241 3290

CANADA: Cook Communications Ministries, PO Box 98, 55 Woodslee Avenue,
Paris, Ontario N3L 3E5.
Tel: 1800 263 2664

GHANA: Challenge Enterprises of Ghana, PO Box 5723, Accra.
Tel: (021) 222437/223249 Fax: (021) 226227

HONG KONG: Cross Communications Ltd, 1/F, 562A Nathan Road, Kowloon.
Tel: 2780 1188 Fax: 2770 6229

INDIA: Crystal Communications, 10-3-18/4/1, East Marredpalli,
Secunderabad – 500026, Andhra Pradesh
Tel/Fax: (040) 27737145

KENYA: Keswick Books and Gifts Ltd, PO Box 10242, Nairobi.
Tel: (02) 331692/226047 Fax: (02) 728557

MALAYSIA: Salvation Book Centre (M) Sdn Bhd, 23 Jalan SS 2/64,
47300 Petaling Jaya, Selangor.
Tel: (03) 78766411/78766797 Fax: (03) 78757066/78756360

NEW ZEALAND: CMC Australasia, PO Box 36015, Lower Hutt.
Tel: 0800 449 408 Fax: 0800 449 049

NIGERIA: FBFM, Helen Baugh House, 96 St Finbarr's College Road,
Akoka, Lagos.
Tel: (01) 7747429/4700218/825775/827264

PHILIPPINES: OMF Literature Inc, 776 Boni Avenue, Mandaluyong City.
Tel: (02) 531 2183 Fax: (02) 531 1960

SINGAPORE: Armour Publishing Pte Ltd, Block 203A Henderson Road,
11-06 Henderson Industrial Park, Singapore 159546.
Tel: 6 276 9976 Fax: 6 276 7564

SOUTH AFRICA: Struik Christian Books, 80 MacKenzie Street, PO Box 1144,
Cape Town 8000.
Tel: (021) 462 4360 Fax: (021) 461 3612

SRI LANKA: Christombu Publications (Pvt) Ltd, Bartleet House,
65 Braybrooke Place, Colombo 2.
Tel: (01) 433142/328909

TANZANIA: CLC Christian Book Centre, PO Box 1384, Mkwepu Street, Dar es Salaam.
Tel/Fax: (022) 2119439

USA: Cook Communications Ministries, PO Box 98, 55 Woodslee Avenue, Paris, Ontario N3L 3E5, Canada.
Tel: 1800 263 2664

ZIMBABWE: Word of Life Books (Pvt) Ltd, Christian Media Centre, 8 Aberdeen Road, Avondale, PO Box A480 Avondale, Harare.
Tel: (04) 333355 or 091301188

For email addresses, visit the CWR website: www.cwr.org.uk

CWR is a registered charity – Number 294387

CWR is a limited company registered in England – Registration Number 1990308

CWR's Ministry to Women

CWR offers an exciting programme of events, seminars and courses to inspire women in their walk with God …

Weekends of Spiritual Refreshing

Opportunities to retreat from the pressures of everyday life and draw closer to God in the beautiful surroundings of Waverley Abbey House.

Day Events at Waverley

Excellent biblical teaching from a variety of guest speakers, with worship, warm fellowship and good food!

Seminars we can bring to your local area

CWR has a range of popular seminars which we are delighted to be able to present in your local church:

- How to be a Secure Woman
- Designer Living
- The Heart of a Woman
- Finding Hope in a Hurting World
- Women Mentoring Women

Women Ministering to Women

Be equipped for ministry through this biblically-based course, for those in any aspect of ministry to women. (Eight Mondays, Jan–Mar.)

Other CWR courses and seminars

CWR offers a wide range of courses, seminars and events, including:

- Day seminars on a wide range of topics to help you to apply God's Word to everyday life and relationships
- Biblical Pastoral Care and Counselling training
- Spiritual Direction and Biblical Coaching training
- Preparation for Marriage weekends
- Bible Discovery Weekends
- Leadership training
- One-week Summer School

For dates/further information: www.cwr.org.uk
Waverley Training and Events, CWR, Waverley Abbey House, Waverley Lane, Farnham, Surrey GU9 8EP

Tel: +44 (0) 1252 784731
Email: training@cwr.org.uk

Waverley
Training and Events

CWR CRUSADE FOR WORLD REVIVAL
Applying God's Word to everyday life and relationships

How to be a Secure Woman

Based on the popular How to be a Secure Woman seminar, this book, featuring eight sessions, is ideal for either personal or group use. Jeannette Barwick and Catherine Butcher help women bridge the gap to become secure women in our insecure world. Using examples of women in the Bible and women today, they offer practical steps that lead to the lasting security found in a relationship with God. An ideal progression or companion to this devotional.

ISBN: 1-85345-307-2
£4.99 (plus p&p)

**How to be a
Secure Woman**
8 Bible-based sessions

Jeannette Barwick and Catherine Butcher

Price correct at time of printing

Inspiring Women Every Day

If you have enjoyed enriching your walk with God by using this *How to be a Secure Woman Devotional*, you may like to continue spending time with God each day with *Inspiring Women Every Day*. This life-enriching daily devotional written for women by women is a source of inspiration and encouragement to all ages.

- Find practical support to face the challenges of living
- Be encouraged by the insightful guidance of Scripture
- Build your faith and inspire your Christian walk with daily readings

ISSN: 1478-050X
£1.99 (plus p&p)
each

or
£11.50 UK annual
subscription
(6 issues inc p&p)

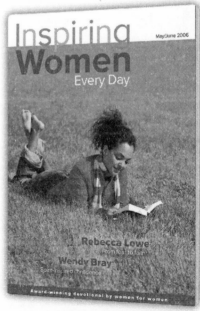

Prices correct at time of printing